Soup Cookbook

Soup Recipes

Served hot or cold, soups are great all year long. Try our nutritious soup recipes that are packed with flavour.

Authentic and modern Soup recipes

Whether you're passionate about Soup cuisine or simply looking to expand your skills in the kitchen and try something new, you will find this Soup Cookbook to be a fascinating and reliable window into Soup cooking and culture.

Thai curry noodle soup

INGREDIENTS

2 tbs coconut oil
2 large desiree potatoes, peeled, cut into 4cm chunks
1 onion, thinly sliced
1/2 cup (150g) yellow curry paste
800ml coconut milk
2 cups (500ml) chicken stock
1/4 cup (60ml) fish sauce
1/2 tsp brown sugar
Juice of 1 lime
600g skinless chicken thigh fillets
200g dried rice noodles, cooked according to packet instructions
2 cups baby spinach
1 long red chilli, thinly sliced
Thai basil leaves plus coriander leaves, to serve

METHOD

1.Heat oil in a large saucepan over high heat and add the potato. Cook, stirring, for 2-3 minutes to soften slightly, then add the onion and cook, stirring, for a further 2-3 minutes or until soft. Add curry paste and stir until fragrant and potato and onion are coated. Stir in the coconut milk, stock and 2 cups (500ml) water until combined. Bring to the boil, then reduce heat to low and simmer for 30 minutes or until potato is just soft.
2.Stir in fish sauce, sugar and lime juice. Check seasoning for balance and add more fish sauce, sugar or lime as required. Cut chicken into 3cm pieces, add to sauce and simmer gently for 25 minutes or until chicken is cooked through
3.To serve, divide the noodles among bowls. Ladle the curry sauce over the noodles and garnish with spinach, chilli Thai basil and coriander to serve.

Bacon and miso pumpkin soup recipe

INGREDIENTS

50g butter, chopped
2 onions, finely chopped
150g smoked streaky bacon rashers, chopped, plus 50g extra whole
3 cloves garlic, crushed
1kg Japanese pumpkin, skinned, seeded and chopped
¼ cup (60ml) mirin
1/3 cup (80g) white miso
4 cups (1 litre) chicken stock
1/3 cup (80ml) sour cream
Chopped chives & chilli flakes, to serve

METHOD

1.Melt butter in a large heavy-based frying pan, add onion and chopped bacon and fry for 5 minutes or until onion softens. Add garlic and pumpkin, cook for a further 3 minutes, then deglaze pan with mirin. Add miso, stock and 1 cup (250ml) water and stir to combine. Bring to the boil, reduce to a simmer and cook, stirring occasionally, for 25 minutes or until pumpkin is soft. Blitz with a stick blender until smooth. Season
2.Heat a small frying pan over medium-low heat, add extra bacon and cook, turning once, for 5 minutes or until crisp. Roughly chop. To serve, divide soup among bowls, top with bacon and a swirl of sour cream and scatter with chives and chilli flakes.

French onion soup with cheese toast

INGREDIENTS

40g unsalted butter (we used Le Conquerant), plus extra to spread
4 large onions, halved, thinly sliced
4 eschalots, thinly sliced
2 thyme sprigs
8 cups (2L) beef bone broth (or any good quality beef stock)
2 tbs sherry or ruby port
1/2 garlic clove
4 slices sourdough bread
1 cup Bruny Island C2 or other hard Alpine cheese, grated

METHOD

1.Melt butter in a large heavy-based saucepan with a lid over medium-low heat. Add onion and eschalot and cook, covered, for 40-50 minutes, stirring frequently, until deep golden and sweet. (You may need to stir more frequently towards the end. Be careful not to burn the onions, as they will become bitter.)

2.Add thyme, stir to combine, then add half the broth and simmer, uncovered, for 15 minutes. Add remaining broth and sherry, and simmer for a further 40 minutes or until the soup is rich and has reduced slightly. Season to taste.

3.Meanwhile, to make the Bruny Island C2 cheese toast, preheat oven to 180°C. Rub garlic over both sides of the sourdough slices and spread with extra butter. Place on an oven tray and bake for 3-4 minutes until lightly toasted.

4.Ladle hot soup into four ovenproof bowls. Top each with a piece of toast, then sprinkle cheese generously and evenly across the top. Switch oven to grill and cook for 2-3 minutes, watching carefully, until cheese is melted, golden and crispy and the soup is bubbling.

Cauliflower, brown butter and pancetta soup

INGREDIENTS

2 tbs extra virgin olive oil
60g unsalted butter
1 onion, finely chopped
1 leek, white and light-green part only, thinly sliced
1 garlic clove, crushed
140g pancetta or speck, skin removed, cut into lardons
1kg cauliflower, cut into florets
6 cups (1.5L) Massel Chicken Style Liquid Stock
1/2 bunch sage, leaves picked
Shaved parmesan, to serve

METHOD

1.Heat oil and 20g butter in a large heavy- based saucepan over medium-high heat. Add onion, leek, garlic and half of the pancetta. Cook, stirring frequently, for 3-4 minutes then add cauliflower and cook for a further 5-6 minutes or until cauliflower and pancetta begin to brown. Add stock, bring to the boil, reduce heat to low and simmer, stirring occasionally, for 1 hour or until vegetables are soft. Transfer soup to a blender (or use a stick blender) and whiz until smooth. Season and keep warm.

2.Meanwhile, add the remaining 70g pancetta to a small, non-stick frypan and cook over high heat, stirring frequently, for 4-6 minutes until golden and crisp. Drain on paper towel and set aside.

3.Place remaining 40g butter in a medium frypan over high heat. When butter begins to foam, add sage. Cook, stirring continuously, for 1-2 minutes until sage is crisp and butter is golden brown.

4.Divide soup among bowls. Drizzle with brown butter and top with crispy pancetta and fried sage. Scatter over parmesan and freshly ground black pepper to serve.

This fast 20-minute soup recipe is your antidote to being hangry

INGREDIENTS

¼ cup (60ml) extra virgin olive oil
50g unsalted butter
5cm piece (25g) ginger, finely grated
1 butternut pumpkin, peeled, coarsely grated
1 tbs curry powder
4 cups (1 litre) Massel Chicken Style Liquid Stock
2 x 400ml cans coconut milk, plus extra to serve (we used Woolworths Macro)
1 bunch coriander, leaves picked, roots washed and chopped

METHOD

1.Heat oil and butter in a large saucepan over medium heat. Add ginger and cook, stirring, for 2 minutes until fragrant. Add pumpkin and stir to coat. Add curry powder and stir to coat the pumpkin. Add stock, coconut milk and coriander root. Bring to the boil and simmer for 10-15 minutes or until pumpkin is tender. Cool slightly, then, in 2 batches, whiz in a blender until smooth. Season to taste.

2.To serve, swirl extra coconut milk through soup. Top with coriander leaves and sprinkle with freshly ground black pepper.

Cauliflower, potato, leek and parmesan soup with gremolata oil

INGREDIENTS

2/3 cup (160ml) extra virgin olive oil
1 cauliflower, trimmed, cut into small florets
2 small potatoes (about 300g), peeled, chopped into 2cm pieces
1 celery stalk, finely chopped
1 leek (white part only), thinly sliced
2 garlic cloves, crushed, plus 1 extra whole garlic clove
4 cups (1L) vegetable or chicken stock
3 cups (750ml) milk
1 parmesan rind, plus 1 1/2 cups (90g) finely grated parmesan
3/4 cup flat-leaf parsley leaves
Pared zest of 1 lemon
Micro parsley & chilli flakes, to serve

METHOD

1.Heat half the oil in a large heavy-based saucepan over medium-high heat. Add cauliflower, potato, celery, leek and crushed garlic, season and cook for 7 minutes, stirring regularly.

2.Add stock, milk and parmesan rind, bring to the boil, reduce to a simmer and cook, stirring regularly, for 20 minutes or until vegetables are soft. Turn off heat and discard parmesan rind. Stir in grated parmesan and transfer to a blender (or use a stick blender) and blitz until very smooth. Season.

3.Meanwhile, to make gremolata oil, place parsley, extra garlic clove and lemon zest on a chopping board and finely chop all together. Place mixture in a small bowl and add remaining 1/3 cup (80ml) oil. Season and stir to combine.

4.Divide soup among serving bowls, spoon over gremolata oil and scatter with micro parsley and a pinch of chilli flakes to serve.

Baked sweet potato soup with blue cheese toast

INGREDIENTS

1kg sweet potato
1 onion (unpeeled), halved
1 garlic bulb, halved crossways
4 cups (1L) vegetable stock
1/2 cup (80g) smoked almonds, chopped
1/2 cup firmly packed mint leaves, finely chopped, plus extra leaves to serve
4 x 1.5cm-thick slices seeded sourdough
120g blue cheese, thinly sliced

METHOD

1.Preheat the oven to 180°C. Grease a baking tray and line with baking paper.
2.Prick sweet potato all over with a fork and place on prepared tray with onion, cut-side down. Roast for 30 minutes, then add garlic, cut-side down, and roast, turning halfway, for a further 1 hour or until vegetables are tender.
3.Remove onion skin and discard. Squeeze garlic flesh from skin into a blender. Working in batches, add onion, sweet potato and stock, and whiz until smooth. Transfer to a saucepan over medium-high heat and cook, stirring occasionally, until hot.
4.Combine almond and mint in a bowl and set aside.
5.Meanwhile, to make the blue cheese toast, preheat oven grill to high and line a baking tray with foil.
6.Place sliced sourdough on prepared tray and grill, checking regularly, for 2 minutes or until toasted. Turn and grill, checking regularly, for 90 seconds or until almost toasted. Top with blue cheese and grill, checking regularly, for 90 seconds or until cheese starts to melt.
7.Divide soup among serving bowls and scatter almond mixture over toast and soup. Top soup with extra mint leaves and serve immediately.

Herby zucchini, leek and potato soup

INGREDIENTS

100ml extra virgin olive oil
50g butter
3 leeks, thinly sliced
2 garlic cloves, finely chopped
1 tbs finely chopped rosemary
600g potatoes, peeled and chopped
3 zucchinis, thinly sliced
6 cups (1.5L) Massel Vegetable Liquid Stock
1 bay leaf
60g finely grated parmesan, plus 1 rind
50g baby spinach leaves
1/2 bunch flat-leaf parsley leaves, chopped
1/4 cup (60g) sour cream
Sourdough croutons, to serve
2 tbs each chopped chives & dill sprigs

METHOD

1.Melt oil and butter together in a large saucepan over low heat. Add leek and 1/2 tsp salt flakes, and cook, stirring, for 25 minutes or until very soft. Add garlic and rosemary, and cook, stirring, for a further 5 minutes or until softened and fragrant.

2.Add potato, zucchini and stock with bay leaf and parmesan rind, and bring to a simmer. Cook for 30 minutes or until potato is very tender. Fold through parmesan, then add spinach and parsley. Remove from the heat and discard parmesan rind.

3.In two batches, transfer soup to a blender and whiz until smooth. Season to taste. Combine sour cream with 1 tbs cold water, to loosen.

4.Divide soup among bowls and drizzle with sour cream. Scatter with croutons, then top with chives, dill and freshly ground black pepper, to serve.

Chickpea, capsicum and prawn soup

INGREDIENTS

2kg red capsicums
2 cups (500ml) Massel Vegetable Liquid Stock
800g canned chickpeas, rinsed, drained
1/4 cup (60ml) extra virgin olive oil
500g peeled green prawns, finely chopped
2 garlic cloves, crushed
Pinch dried chilli flakes
1 tsp smoked paprika (pimenton)

METHOD

1.Preheat the oven grill to high. Place capsicums on a baking tray and grill, checking regularly and turning halfway, for 15-18 minutes or until blackened and tender. Transfer to a bowl, cover with plastic wrap and stand for 10 minutes to steam. Peel capsicums, discarding tops and seeds, and halve. Reserve capsicum resting liquid.

2.Transfer capsicum flesh and resting liquid to a blender with stock and whiz until smooth. Transfer to a saucepan over high heat and bring to a simmer. Reduce heat to low to keep hot.

3.Spread chickpeas over a tray and pat dry with paper towel.

4.Heat half the oil in a large frypan over high heat. Add prawn and cook, stirring occasionally, for 3 minutes or until just cooked through, then transfer to a bowl. Add remaining 11/2 tbs oil to pan with chickpeas, garlic and chilli, and cook, stirring occasionally, for 3 minutes or until heated through and starting to turn golden. Add prawn, smoked paprika, 1/2 tsp salt flakes and 1/2 cup (125ml) capsicum soup, and cook, stirring constantly, for 1 minute or until fragrant.

5.Divide chickpea mixture and remaining soup among bowls and serve immediately.

Chicken, silken tofu and cabbage soup

INGREDIENTS

4 chicken thigh fillets
2 tbs red miso paste (from selected supermarkets)
1/2 small green cabbage, cut into 4 pieces
8 spring onions, trimmed, halved
2 long red chillies, halved lengthways
1 tsp shichimi togarashi (from Asian food shops and selected supermarkets),
plus extra to serve
2 tbs white soy sauce (from Asian food shops – substitute light soy sauce)
4cm piece (20g) ginger, finely grated
2 tbs rice vinegar
2 tbs mirin
2 x 300g packets silken tofu, halved
Micro radish leaves and toasted seasoned nori sheets, to serve

METHOD

1.In a large saucepan carefully layer the chicken, miso paste, cabbage, spring onion and chilli, and sprinkle with shichimi togarashi. Add soy sauce, then gently pour 2L (8 cups) water down the inside of the pan, being careful not to disturb the layers.

2.Place saucepan over high heat and bring to the boil. Reduce to a simmer and cook, without stirring, for 35-45 minutes or until cabbage is tender and chicken is cooked through. Set aside to cool slightly.

3.Meanwhile, combine the ginger, vinegar and mirin in a bowl and set aside.

4.Remove chicken and shred roughly with two forks. Divide tofu pieces among 4 bowls. Add cabbage pieces, chicken, spring onion and chilli, then pour over broth.

5.Sprinkle with extra shichimi togarashi and top with the micro radish, toasted nori and ginger dressing to serve.

Chicken hot and sour soup with pumpkin

INGREDIENTS

1kg Queensland Blue pumpkin
6 free-range chicken thighs, skin off, bone out
Groundnut oil
2.5cm piece of ginger
2 cloves of garlic
3 fresh red chillies
1 stick of lemongrass
3 kaffir lime leaves
600ml organic chicken stock
1 x 400g tin of light coconut milk
150g oyster mushrooms
2 limes
1 bunch of fresh Thai basil (30g)
2 tablespoons fish sauce
1 tablespoon palm sugar or soft brown sugar
Optional: 1 punnet of micro cress

METHOD

1.Trim and peel the pumpkin, cut in half lengthways, then scoop out and discard the seeds. Chop the pumpkin and chicken thighs into 3cm chunks.
2.Drizzle 1 tablespoon of oil into a large pan over a medium heat, add the chicken and cook for 5 minutes or until golden, stirring regularly.
3.Peel and finely grate the ginger and garlic. Finely slice two of the chillies and bash the lemongrass with the back of a knife. Stir into the pan, then toss in the lime leaves. Cook everything for a further 2 minutes, or until the ginger and garlic has softened, stirring regularly.
4.Add the pumpkin to the pan, then pour in the stock and coconut milk, and stir well. Bring to the boil, reduce the heat to low and simmer for 25-30 minutes or until the pumpkin is tender and the sauce has thickened, tearing in the mushrooms after 15 minutes.
5.Finely slice the remaining chilli. Cut 1 lime into wedges and pick the Thai basil leaves, discarding the stalks.
6.Remove the soup from the heat and stir in the fish sauce. Add the palm or brown sugar, squeeze in the juice from the remaining lime and season to perfection with sea salt and black pepper.
7.Divide the hot soup between warm bowls, then scatter over the chilli and basil. Snip over the cress (if using) and serve with lime wedges on the side for squeezing over.

Chicken noodle soup with sesame and ginger

INGREDIENTS

1.6kg (size 16) whole free-range chicken
1 tbs sesame oil, plus extra to serve
1 onion
2 carrots, halved
2 celery stalks, chopped
5cm piece ginger, sliced
150g dried egg noodles
3 tbs chopped flat-leaf parsley
1 tbs light soy sauce
4-6 spring onions, thinly sliced

METHOD

1.Rub chicken all over with the sesame oil. Place in a large saucepan with vegetables, ginger and 3 litres of cold water. Bring to the boil, skimming surface to remove any fat or impurities. Reduce heat to medium low and simmer uncovered for 1 hour. Remove chicken, then strain soup into a clean pan, discarding vegetables. Return soup to boil, add noodles and cook for 5 minutes.

2.Meanwhile, shred chicken when cool enough to handle, discarding skin and bones. Add meat to cooked noodles with parsley and soy. Season to taste, then serve topped with spring onion and drizzled with a little extra sesame oil.

Chicken noodle soup

INGREDIENTS

1 (about 1.4kg) organic chicken
1 onion, peeled
1 garlic clove
2 carrots, peeled, chopped
2 celery stalks, leaves removed
1 bay leaf
2 sprigs thyme
200g vermicelli pasta, cooked, drained
2 tablespoons freshly chopped flat-leaf parsley

METHOD

1.Place the chicken in a large saucepan with the onion, garlic, carrots, celery, herbs and 2 litres of water. Bring to the boil, skimming any scum that may appear on the surface. Reduce heat to very low and simmer for 2 hours (don't boil). Strain the soup, returning the liquid to the pan. Set aside the chicken to cool, discard vegetables.

2.When the chicken is cool enough to handle, remove the meat from the bones and set aside to use in other dishes. Return the bones to the stock and cook for a further hour at a low simmer. Strain, allow to cool, then refrigerate overnight.

3.Remove any fat that has appeared on the surface and discard. Reheat soup. Season well with salt and pepper.

4.Divide pasta between serving bowls, and ladle the soup over the top. Sprinkle with parsley and serve.

Chicken meatball soup

INGREDIENTS

1/2 cup each firmly packed basil and flat-leaf parsley leaves, plus extra small
basil leaves to serve
500g chicken mince
1 eggwhite
5 garlic cloves, finely grated
2 onions, peeled, coarsely grated
2 tbs olive oil, plus extra to drizzle
2 x 400g cans crushed tomatoes
1L (4 cups) chicken stock
Finely grated and shaved parmesan, to serve

METHOD

1.To make the meatballs, whiz basil and parsley in a food processor until
finely chopped. Add chicken, eggwhite, half the grated garlic and half the
onion, and pulse until just combined. Leave mixture in bowl and chill until
required.
2.Place oil and remaining garlic and onion in a saucepan over high heat and
cook, stirring, for 2 minutes or until onion begins to soften. Stir through
tomatoes and stock, and remove from heat. Using a stick blender, whiz
tomato mixture until smooth. Return pan to high heat.
3.Meanwhile, with wet hands, roll tablespoon-sized balls of chicken mixture
into meatballs and add to soup. With soup at a simmer, swirl pan, then cover
and cook, carefully stirring twice, for 8 minutes or until meatballs are
cooked through.
4.Divide soup among bowls, scatter with parmesan and extra basil leaves,
and drizzle with extra oil to serve.

Chicken and egg noodle soup

INGREDIENTS

4 dried shiitake mushrooms
250g fresh egg noodles
2 bunches baby bok choy, trimmed
2 cups (320g) shredded cooked chicken
1.5L (6 cups) chicken stock
1 tbs dark soy sauce
11/2 tbs white sugar
1 tbs fish sauce
2 tbs lime juice
Thai basil leaves, to serve
Sliced red chilli, to serve
Bean sprouts, to serve
Lime wedges, to serve

METHOD

1.Place shiitakes in a heatproof bowl and cover with boiling water. Set aside to soak for 10 minutes. Drain, remove stalks and thinly slice, reserving 2 tbs soaking liquid.
2.Prepare the egg noodles according to packet instructions, then drain and divide among 4 serving bowls. Top with the bok choy and chicken.
3.Bring stock to a boil in a saucepan over high heat. Add shiitakes, reserved liquid, soy sauce, sugar, fish sauce and lime juice. Ladle broth into bowls, and top with basil, chilli and sprouts. Serve with lime.

Cauliflower soup with brioche crumbs

INGREDIENTS

50g unsalted butter
1 onion, chopped
1 cauliflower, cut into florets
2 cups (500ml) chicken or vegetable stock
300ml milk
300ml pure (thin) cream
1 small brioche, torn
1 garlic clove, roughly chopped
1 tablespoon finely chopped flat-leaf parsley

METHOD

1.Melt butter in a large saucepan over medium-low heat. Cook the onion for 3-4 minutes until soft but not coloured. Add cauliflower and cook, stirring, for 1 minute. Add stock and milk, then bring to the boil. Reduce the heat to low and cook for 5-6 minutes until cauliflower is tender. Cool slightly, then blend soup until smooth. Return to pan with cream and heat through. Season with sea salt and white pepper.

2.Meanwhile, preheat the oven to 180°C. Process brioche and garlic in a food processor to form crumbs. Spread on a baking tray and toast for 5-6 minutes until golden, then toss with parsley. Serve soup sprinkled with the crumbs.

Cauliflower cream of chicken soup

INGREDIENTS

2L (8 cups) Massel Chicken Style Liquid Stock
1kg cauliflower (about 1 medium head, trimmed), cut into florets
1 cup (250ml) pure (thin) cream
2 skinless chicken breasts (we used Woolworths Macro)
Micro coriander, to serve
SPICY CAULIFLOWER SPRINKLE
1/2 tsp coriander seeds, toasted
1 jalapeno, finely chopped
2 cauliflower florets, finely chopped
2 tbs toasted cashews, finely chopped

METHOD

1.Place stock in a saucepan with a lid over high heat and bring to boil. Add cauliflower and cook, covered, for 10-12 minutes or until cauliflower is tender. In batches, transfer to a blender and whiz until smooth.
2.Return soup base to a clean saucepan with a lid over medium heat and add cream and chicken. Cover and simmer gently for 10 minutes or until chicken is cooked through.
3.Remove chicken using a slotted spoon and cut into thick slices. Return chicken to the soup and keep warm over low heat until ready to serve.
4.Meanwhile, for the spicy cauliflower sprinkle, using a mortar and pestle, pound coriander seeds until coarsely ground. Transfer to a bowl and add jalapeno, cauliflower and cashews. Stir to combine.
5.Divide soup among bowls and top with the spiced cauliflower sprinkle. Scatter with micro coriander to serve.

Cauliflower cheese soup (vegetarian)

INGREDIENTS

700g cauliflower
450ml milk
450ml thin cream
1 bay leaf
50g unsalted butter
350g chopped onion
25g plain flour
200ml vegetable stock
350g cheddar or gruyere cheese (or half & half)
1/2 teaspoon grated nutmeg

METHOD

1.Chop cauliflower into small florets, discard outer leaves and place in a pan with milk, cream and bay leaf. Simmer over low heat until tender. Strain, reserving cauliflower and liquid.

2.Wipe pan clean, return to heat and melt butter. Add onion and cook over low heat for 5 minutes or until just softened. Add flour and cook for 1 minute, then add stock and strained liquid, stirring to combine. Cook for 1-2 minutes over a low to medium heat or until slightly thickened.

3.Add cauliflower and 300g of cheese and season with salt, pepper and nutmeg. (Soup can be prepared ahead up to this stage and kept refrigerated.)

4.Preheat the oven to 220°C.

5.Divide soup between 6 ovenproof serving bowls and sprinkle with remaining cheese. Place bowls in a roasting pan, pour in enough water to come halfway up the sides of bowls and bake for 10-15 minutes or until cheese is bubbling and golden.

Cauliflower and parsnip soup with parmesan croutons

INGREDIENTS

1/4 cup (60ml) olive oil
1 onion, roughly chopped
3 garlic cloves, roughly chopped
1kg parsnips, peeled, cut into 3cm pieces
1 small cauliflower, cut into florets
1 long green chilli, seeds removed, finely chopped
1/8 teaspoon cayenne pepper
1/4 teaspoon sweet paprika
2L (8 cups) vegetable stock
4 thick slices sourdough bread, crusts removed, torn into 3cm pieces
2/3 cup (50g) grated parmesan
Pure (thin) cream & finely chopped flat-leaf parsley or chives, to serve

METHOD

1.Heat 1 tablespoon oil in a large saucepan over medium heat. Add onion and garlic, then cook, stirring, for 3-4 minutes until softened. Add parsnip and cauliflower, then cook for 15-20 minutes or until starting to soften and slightly caramelised.

2.Add chilli, cayenne, paprika and stock, scraping bottom of the pan with a spoon, then cook, stirring, for 10-15 minutes until the vegetables are tender. Season.

3.Transfer to a blender and whiz until smooth. Return soup to the pan, season, then keep warm over medium heat.

4.Meanwhile, preheat the oven to 220°C. Place bread on a baking tray and drizzle with remaining 2 tablespoons oil. Bake for 7 minutes or until slightly toasted, then sprinkle over parmesan and bake for a further 5 minutes or until golden.

5.To serve, swirl cream through soup and garnish with herbs and croutons.

Carrot and ginger soup with French-style lentils

INGREDIENTS

6 large carrots, roughly chopped
1/2 teaspoon fennel seeds
1/4 cup (60ml) olive oil
1 onion, chopped
3 garlic cloves, thinly sliced
2 celery stalks, chopped
3cm piece ginger, grated
3 thyme sprigs, leaves picked, plus extra sprigs to serve
1.5L (6 cups) vegetable stock
1 cup (200g) dried green Puy-style lentils
Crusty bread, to serve

METHOD

1.Preheat the oven to 180°C and line a baking tray with baking paper.
2.Place carrot, fennel and 2 tablespoons oil in a bowl, then season and toss. Tip onto tray and roast for 30 minutes or until tender.
3.Heat the remaining 1 tablespoon oil in a large saucepan over medium heat. Add the onion and garlic, then cook, stirring, for 3-4 minutes until softened. Add the celery and cook for 3-4 minutes until softened. Add the ginger, thyme, stock and roasted carrot, then cook, stirring occasionally, for 25-30 minutes until liquid is slightly reduced. Transfer to a blender and whiz until smooth. Return the soup to the pan and set aside.
4.Meanwhile, place the lentils and 2 1/2 cups (625ml) cold water in a saucepan. Bring to the boil, then reduce heat to low and cook for 30 minutes or until liquid is absorbed and lentils are tender.
5.Stir the lentils through the soup and cook over medium heat for 2 minutes or until warmed through. Remove from heat.
6.Garnish the soup with extra thyme sprigs and serve with warm chunks of bread.

Carrot and chorizo soup

INGREDIENTS

30g unsalted butter
1 tablespoon olive oil
2 onions, finely chopped
2 garlic cloves, finely chopped
5 coriander roots, plus leaves to serve
2 teaspoons ground coriander
1 teaspoon ground turmeric
3 teaspoons cumin seeds
1kg carrots, chopped
1.25L (5 cups) Massel Chicken Style Liquid Stock
1 tablespoon lemon juice
150g chorizo, finely chopped

METHOD

1.Heat the butter and oil in a large saucepan over medium-low heat. Cook the onion and garlic, stirring, for 5-6 minutes until softened. Add the coriander roots, ground coriander, turmeric and 2 teaspoons cumin seeds and cook, stirring, for 1-2 minutes until fragrant. Add carrot, then cover and cook, stirring occasionally, for 10 minutes until starting to soften. Season, then add stock. Bring to the boil, then reduce heat to medium and simmer for 20 minutes or until the carrots are tender. Cool slightly, then blend, in batches, until smooth. Stir through the lemon juice.

2.Meanwhile, heat a non-stick frypan over medium heat. Add the chorizo and remaining 1 teaspoon cumin seeds and cook, stirring, for 3-4 minutes until crisp.

3.Divide soup among bowls and serve with chorizo and coriander leaves.

Broccoli and gruyere soup with garlic cheese toasts

INGREDIENTS

15g unsalted butter
1 tbs olive oil
1 large onion, chopped
1 garlic clove, crushed
800g broccoli (2 large heads), trimmed, fl orets roughly chopped (you should
have 600g chopped fl orets)
1L (4 cups) chicken or vegetable stock
1/4 cup (60ml) pure (thin) cream, plus extra to serve
1/2 cup (70g) grated gruyere cheese
GARLIC CHEESE TOASTS
2 garlic cloves, crushed
40g unsalted butter, softened
1 baguette, cut into 4 pieces, each halved lengthways
1/2 cup finely grated cheese (such as parmesan or gruyere)

METHOD

1.Heat butter and oil in a large heavy-based saucepan over medium heat.
Add the onion and cook, stirring occasionally, for 5-6 minutes until soft. Add
the garlic and cook, stirring, for a further minute.
2.Add the broccoli and stock and bring to the boil over high heat. Reduce
heat to medium-low and simmer, partially covered, for 5-6 minutes until
broccoli is tender. Set aside to cool slightly.
3.For the garlic cheese toasts, preheat oven to 180°C. Use a fork to mash the
garlic and butter until well combined.
4.Spread the baguette with garlic butter, place on a baking tray and bake for
5 minutes. Remove from the oven, sprinkle with cheese and bake for a
further 3-4 minutes until cheese melts.
5.Puree soup in a blender, in batches, until smooth. Return to the pan and
season with sea salt and freshly ground black pepper. Add the cream and
gruyere and stir over medium heat until heated through. Ladle soup among
bowls, swirl in a spoonful of extra cream. Serve with garlic cheese toasts.

Chunky tomato, celery and bean soup

INGREDIENTS

2 tablespoons olive oil, plus 1 tablespoon extra to drizzle
1 large onion, finely chopped
2 celery stalks, finely chopped
1 tablespoon chopped fresh rosemary leaves
2 garlic cloves, finely chopped
2 x 400g cans cannellini beans, rinsed, drained
2 cups (500ml) chicken or vegetable stock
5 tomatoes (750g total), chopped
2 tablespoons chopped flat-leaf parsley leaves
4 wholegrain bread rolls, to serve

METHOD

1.Heat oil in a large pan over medium heat. Add onion, celery, rosemary and garlic and stir for 5 minutes until vegetables soften. Add beans, stock and tomatoes. Season with salt and pepper, bring to the boil over high heat, then reduce heat to low, cover and gently simmer for 15 minutes or until thickened. Stir in parsley, then spoon soup into bowls. Drizzle with extra oil and serve with bread rolls.

Chicken turmeric soup

INGREDIENTS

2 x 180g chicken breasts
1 tbs sunflower oil, plus extra to brush
200g vermicelli noodles, cooked according to packet instructions
Thinly sliced long red chilli, to serve
Sliced spring onions, to serve
Sliced chives, to serve
Mint leaves, to serve
TURMERIC SPICE PASTE
1 tbs finely grated galangal
1 1/2 tbs finely grated turmeric
2 small red chillies, chopped
6 candlenuts (hard, oily tropical nut – from Herbie's Spices) or 12 macadamias
3 lemongrass stalks (inner core only), finely grated
6 red (Asian) eschalots, chopped
5 kaffir lime leaves, shredded
4 garlic cloves, chopped
2 tbs sunflower oil
2 tbs sesame oil
TUMERIC LEMONGRASS BROTH
1.5L (6 cups) chicken stock
11/2 tbs tamarind puree
1/4 cup (60ml) fish sauce
Juice of 1 lime
1 tbs palm sugar, grated
2 kaffir lime leaves
1/2 tsp freshly ground white pepper

METHOD

1.For the spice paste, whiz all ingredients in a food processor until a paste.
2.Cut chicken in half lengthways. Rub 2 tbs spice paste into chicken. Chill for 1 hour.
3.Heat oil in a pan over medium heat. Add remaining spice paste and cook, stirring occasionally, for 4-5 minutes until fragrant.
4.Add all the broth ingredients, except the pepper, and bring to the boil. Reduce heat to low and simmer for 10 minutes or until slightly reduced.
5.Strain, discarding solids. When ready to serve, reheat broth in a clean saucepan and stir through pepper.
6.Brush a chargrill pan with oil and place over high heat. Grill chicken for 2 minutes each side or until cooked through. Cut chicken into thin strips.
7.Divide noodles and broth among bowls. Top with chicken, chilli, spring onion, chives and mint to serve.

Chorizo, potato and cabbage soup

INGREDIENTS

2 chorizo sausages
1 red onion, peeled, halved
2 cloves of garlic, peeled
1 red paprika, deseeded (or red capsicum)
700g water
2 tbsp chicken stock powder
1 tbsp umami paste
1 tbsp ground paprika
500g potatoes, peeled, cubed into bite sized pieces
1 small cabbage (enough for your family, don't go overboard),
cut into thin wedges
1 x 400g tin of chickpeas,
or soaked and cooked equivalent
chopped coriander and/or parsley to garnish

METHOD

1. Place chorizo, onion, garlic and paprika into the Thermomix bowl and chop
3 sec/speed 6. Saute 5 min/Varoma/speed 1.
2. Add all remaining ingredients other than cabbage and chickpeas.
3. Place cabbage into Varoma dish and set into position. Cook 15
min/Varoma/Reverse/speed 1. Set cabbage aside.
4. Add chickpeas to the Thermomix bowl and cook 2
min/100°C/Reverse/speed 1
5. Place wedges of cabbage into large soup bowls and ladle soup over.
Sprinkle with chopped coriander, parsley or both.

Chorizo and vegetable soup

INGREDIENTS

1 tablespoon olive oil
1 onion, roughly chopped
2 garlic cloves, crushed
2 chorizo sausages, sliced
1L (4 cups) chicken stock
800g pontiac potatoes, peeled, cut into 2cm chunks
1 bunch silverbeet, trimmed, sliced
Crusty bread, to serve

METHOD

1.Heat oil in a large saucepan on medium-high heat. Cook onion, garlic and chorizo, stirring, for 5 minutes until onion is soft.
2.Add stock, 1L water and potatoes. Bring to the boil, simmer over medium heat for 12 minutes until potatoes are tender, then add silverbeet. Cook for 2 minutes until just wilted. Season. Serve with bread.

Chilli bean soup

INGREDIENTS

1 tablespoon vegetable oil
1 onion, chopped
300g beef mince
1 teaspoon ground cumin
1 teaspoon ground coriander
Pinch of cayenne
1 teaspoon hot paprika
1 red capsicum, finely chopped
1/2 teaspoon dried oregano
1 cup (250ml) tomato juice
400g can chopped tomatoes
400g can red kidney beans, rinsed, drained

METHOD

1.Heat the vegetable oil in a non-stick frypan over medium-high heat. Add
the onion and cook, stirring, for 5 minutes or until soft.
2.Add the beef mince and spices and cook for 5-6 minutes, breaking up the
mince with a spoon, until the mince browns.
3.Add the capsicum, oregano, tomato juice, tomatoes, 3 cups (750ml) water,
season with sea salt and freshly ground black pepper. Bring to the boil,
stirring, then simmer, covered, over medium-low heat for 20 minutes.
4.Add the kidney beans and simmer for 10 minutes. For a thicker soup, mash
a few of the beans and stir through. Serve in four warm bowls.

Chilli bean soup

INGREDIENTS

1/4 cup (60ml) olive oil
1 onion, roughly chopped
1 red capsicum, roughly chopped
1 celery stalk, roughly chopped
1/2 dried red chilli (see note)
1/2 teaspoon smoked paprika(pimenton)
1 bay leaf
400g can chopped tomatoes
400g can kidney beans, rinsed, drained
1 tablespoon hot chilli sauce
800ml vegetable stock
1 corn tortilla, cut into strips
Lemon juice, to serve

SALSA

Small handful cherry tomatoes (about 50g), chopped
3 coriander sprigs, leaves chopped
1/4 cucumber, seeds removed, chopped
1 tablespoon extra virgin olive oil

METHOD

1.Heat 1 tablespoon oil in a saucepan over medium heat. Throw in the onion, capsicum, celery, dried chilli, paprika and bay leaf, then give it a good stir. Reduce the heat to low, then pop the lid on, slightly askew, and cook for 10 minutes or until the vegies are soft.

2.Stir through the tomatoes, beans, chilli sauce and stock, then increase heat to medium and cook for 10 minutes or until slightly reduced. Remove from heat, discard the bay leaf, then season.

3.Meanwhile, heat the remaining 2 tablespoons oil in a large frypan over medium-high heat. Once hot (test with a corner of tortilla), fry the tortilla strips, in batches if necessary, until crisp and golden. Remove with a slotted spoon and drain on paper towel.

4.To make the salsa, combine the ingredients in a bowl and set aside.

5.Whiz the soup with a stick blender (not too smooth, a few lumps are good), pour into a bowl and top with the tortilla strips, salsa and lemon juice.

Chilled tomato and herb soup

INGREDIENTS

8 vine-ripened tomatoes, halved
2 garlic cloves, thinly sliced
1/4 cup (60ml) olive oil, plus extra to drizzle
1/2 bunch basil, leaves picked
180g sourdough bread, crusts removed, torn
2 tbs red wine vinegar
1 small red onion, quartered
1 red capsicum, chopped
1 long red chilli, seeds removed, chopped
2 tbs oregano leaves, plus extra to serve
6 thin slices (60g) jamon or prosciutto
1/2 cup (120g) sour cream
2 tbs milk

METHOD

1.Preheat the oven to 140C. Line a baking tray with baking paper.
2.Place tomato, cut-side up, on the tray, sprinkle over the garlic, then season and drizzle with oil. Scatter over half the basil, then roast for 2 hours or until the tomato starts to collapse. Cool for 10 minutes, then discard basil.
3.Place bread in a bowl with vinegar and 2 tbs water, and toss to coat. Set aside for 10 minutes or until the liquid is absorbed, then transfer to a blender with the onion, capsicum, chilli, oregano, cooled tomato and remaining basil leaves, and whiz until smooth. Add 11/2 cups (325ml) cold water and whiz to combine. Season, transfer to a jug and chill completely.
4.Meanwhile, increase oven to 180C. Line a baking tray with baking paper and place ham on the tray, then roast for 10-12 minutes until crisp.
5.Combine the sour cream and milk. Ladle chilled tomato soup into bowls, drizzle with sour cream mixture and extra oil, then top each with a crisp slice of ham and extra oregano.

Chilled pea soup with mint gelato

INGREDIENTS

2 cups (240g) frozen peas, plus extra blanched peas to garnish
1 potato, peeled, chopped
1 small onion, finely chopped
1 cup (60g) shredded iceberg lettuce
1L (4 cups) chicken or vegetable stock
1/4 cup (60ml) thickened cream
MINT GELATO
2 teaspoons grated lemon zest, plus 1 tablespoon juice
1/4 cup (55g) caster sugar
1 cup chopped mint leaves, plus whole leaves to garnish
1/2 cup (125g) mascarpone cheese
1 eggwhite

METHOD

1.For the gelato, place lemon zest and juice, sugar and all but 2 tablespoons chopped mint in a pan with 1/3 cup (80ml) water. Stir over low heat to dissolve the sugar. Increase heat to medium and simmer for 2 minutes, then strain through a sieve, pressing down on the solids to extract maximum flavour. Cool, then stir syrup into mascarpone.
2.Transfer the gelato mixture to a shallow plastic container, then place in the freezer for 3 hours or until frozen.
3.Whiz the gelato mixture, eggwhite and reserved 2 tablespoons mint in a food processor until combined. Return to the freezer and freeze for at least 4 hours or overnight.
4.Place peas, potato, onion, lettuce and stock in a pan and bring to the boil. Reduce heat to low and simmer for 10 minutes. Remove from the heat and use a hand blender to puree until smooth. (Alternatively, cool slightly, then puree in a blender in batches, until smooth.) Strain through a sieve, then stir in the cream. Season, then chill for 2-3 hours.
5.When ready to serve, divide the soup among bowls and top with a scoop of gelato and a few mint leaves and peas.

Chilled pea soup with lobster and risoni salad

INGREDIENTS

1 tablespoon unsalted butter
1/4 cup (60ml) extra virgin olive oil
1 leek, white part only, thinly sliced
500g fresh or frozen peas
1 potato, peeled, chopped
3 cups (750ml) chicken stock
1/2 cup (125ml) thin cream
200g risoni*
1 tablespoon chopped chives
1 tablespoon chopped chervil or flat-leaf parsley
2 tablespoons lemon juice
1 tablespoon preserved lemon*, pith and pulp removed, finely chopped
1 small cooked lobster

METHOD

1.Heat butter and 1 tablespoon olive oil in a saucepan, add leek and cook over a low heat until soft but not coloured. Add 400g of peas, the potato and stock and season with salt and pepper. Bring to the boil and simmer for 10 minutes or until potato is cooked. Cool slightly, then puree in a blender. Stir in cream and refrigerate.

2.Cook the risoni in boiling salted water according to the packet instructions, adding the reserved peas for the last 2 minutes of cooking time. Drain, rinse in cold water, drain again. Place in a bowl with herbs, remaining oil, the lemon juice and preserved lemon. Taste for seasoning. Remove lobster meat from the shell, slice into medallions and add to salad. Season well. Place a mound of the salad in each bowl and pour chilled soup around.

Chilled pea and lettuce soup

INGREDIENTS

2 cups (500ml) vegetable or chicken stock
200ml pure (thin) cream, plus extra to serve
1 small potato, peeled, finely chopped
25g unsalted butter, chopped
1 tbs olive oil
2 eschalots, finely chopped
2 garlic cloves, finely chopped
1 baby cos lettuce, washed, chopped
1 2/3 cups (200g) frozen peas
100g baby spinach leaves
1 cup loosely packed flat-leaf parsley leaves
Snow pea tendrils and mint leaves, to serve

METHOD

1.Place stock, cream and potato in a small saucepan over high heat. Bring to the boil.
2.Meanwhile, heat butter and oil in a separate saucepan over medium heat. Add eschalot and garlic, and cook, stirring occasionally, for 4 minutes or until eschalot has softened. Add lettuce, peas, spinach, parsley and boiling stock mixture. Return to the boil, then, working quickly, transfer to a blender and whiz until smooth. Pour soup through a fine sieve into a bowl placed over a larger bowl of ice. Stir to quickly chill. Season to taste.
3.Divide soup among serving bowls and drizzle with extra cream. Scatter with snow pea tendrils and mint leaves to serve.

Chilled pea and avocado soup

INGREDIENTS

1 vegetable stock cube
450g fresh or frozen, thawed peas
1 avocado, roughly chopped
1/3 cup (80ml) thickened cream, plus extra to serve
2 garlic cloves, chopped
1/2 cup mint leaves, plus extra to serve
2 tablespoons lemon juice

METHOD

1.Dissolve stock cube in a jug with 650ml boiling water. Cool slightly.
2.Place cooled stock in a blender with peas, avocado, cream, garlic and mint.
Blend until smooth. Stir in lemon juice, then season. Chill for 1 hour.
3.Divide chilled soup among small cups or bowls, swirl through a little extra
cream and top with extra mint leaves to serve.

Chilled corn soup with drunken tequila prawns

INGREDIENTS

30g unsalted butter
2 tablespoons olive oil
1 onion, finely chopped
2 garlic cloves, finely chopped
6 corn cobs, kernels sliced
3 cups (750ml) chicken stock
1/4 cup (60ml) pure (thin) cream
8 green prawns, peeled (tails intact), deveined
1 cup (250ml) tequila blanco (see note)
Finely grated zest and juice of 1 lime
Thinly sliced red chilli and mustard cress, to serve

METHOD

1.Heat butter and oil in a saucepan over medium heat. Cook onion and garlic, stirring, for 3-4 minutes until softened, but not coloured. Add corn kernels and cook, stirring, for 2 minutes, then add the stock and bring to a simmer. Cook for 15 minutes or until the corn is tender.
2.Cool slightly, then blend soup until smooth. Strain through a sieve into a bowl, pressing down on the solids to extract as much liquid as possible. Stir through the cream and season. Place in the fridge for 2-3 hours until chilled.
3.Meanwhile, bring a pan of salted water to the boil. Add the prawns, then remove immediately from the heat. Stand for 10 minutes, then drain. Place prawns in a bowl with tequila and lime zest and juice, then season. Cool, then transfer to the fridge to marinate for 2 hours.
4.To serve, divide soup among bowls. Drain prawns, then place 2 in each bowl. Season, then garnish with chilli and cress.

Chilled carrot and ginger soup

INGREDIENTS

10g unsalted butter
2 teaspoons olive oil
1 small onion, finely chopped
4cm piece ginger, peeled, grated
6 large carrots (about 600g), halved lengthways, cut into 1cm pieces
3 cups (750ml) reduced-sodium chicken stock
1/4 cup (60ml) lime juice
Coriander sprigs and lime wedges, to serve

METHOD

1.Melt the butter with the oil in a large saucepan over medium-low heat. Cook onion, ginger and carrot, stirring, for 10 minutes. Add stock and 3 cups (750ml) water.
2.Bring to the boil over medium-high heat, then reduce heat to medium and simmer for 10 minutes or until carrot softens. Cool slightly, then puree in a blender, in batches, until smooth. Refrigerate until chilled.
3.To serve, stir in lime juice, sprinkle with freshly ground black pepper and garnish with coriander sprigs. Serve with lime wedges, and rice cakes spread with avocado if desired.

French onion soup

INGREDIENTS

50g unsalted butter
1 teaspoon olive oil
4 large onions (about 1kg), sliced
1 tablespoon brown sugar
50ml brandy
3 cups (750ml) chicken stock
1 tablespoon balsamic vinegar
2 bay leaves
2 thyme sprigs
4 thick slices sourdough
1 garlic clove, halved
1 cup (120g) grated Gruyère cheese

METHOD

1.Melt the butter with the oil in a large saucepan over medium-low heat. Add the onion, sugar and 1 teaspoon salt and cook, stirring occasionally, for 20 minutes or until golden and caramelised.
2.Add the brandy, then increase heat to medium-high and cook for 1-2 minutes until liquid is almost evaporated. Add the chicken stock, balsamic and herbs, bring to a simmer, then reduce heat to low. Cook for 10-15 minutes, stirring occasionally, until thickened.
3.Meanwhile, preheat the grill to high.
4.Grill bread on both sides until golden. Rub one side of each slice with garlic, top with cheese, then grill for a further 1-2 minutes until the cheese has melted.
5.Divide toasts among 4 soup bowls, then ladle over the soup and serve.

Flu-busting super greens soup with truffle oil

INGREDIENTS

1 tbs extra virgin olive oil
1 onion, finely chopped
3 garlic cloves, chopped
1 bunch flat-leaf parsley, stalks chopped, leaves reserved
1 zucchini, thinly sliced
1 fennel bulb, roughly chopped
2 celery stalks, finely chopped
1 head broccoli, stalk chopped, separated into florets
1 bay leaf
2L (8 cups) vegetable stock
400g can chickpeas, drained
300g baby spinach leaves
Juice of 1 lemon
Thick Greek-style yoghurt, to serve
Truffle oil, to serve

METHOD

1.Heat the olive oil in a large saucepan over medium-high heat. Add the onion, garlic, parsley stalks, zucchini, fennel, celery, broccoli stalk and bay leaf, and cook, stirring occasionally, for 10 minutes or until vegetables have softened.

2.Increase heat to high. Add the stock and chickpeas, bring to the boil and boil for 5 minutes. Add broccoli florets, parsley leaves and baby spinach, reduce heat to medium and cook for 5 minutes or until the broccoli is tender.

3.Remove the bay leaf and discard. Puree the soup using a stick blender until smooth. Stir through the lemon juice and season to taste.

4.Divide the soup among bowls. Top with a generous dollop of thick Greek-style yoghurt and season with freshly ground black pepper. Serve soup with a drizzle of truffle oil.

Curried red lentil and coconut soup

INGREDIENTS

1½ tbs coconut oil
1 onion, finely sliced
2 garlic cloves, crushed
1 tbs ginger, finely grated
½ bunch coriander, roots and stalks washed and finely chopped, leaves
picked and roughly chopped, plus extra small leaves to serve
2 tbs red curry paste
1 tbs palm sugar, finely grated
2½ cups (500g) red lentils
4 cups (1L) vegetable stock
400ml can coconut milk
2 tbs fish sauce
Juice of 1 lime
Chopped red chilli and toasted coconut flakes (optional), to serve

METHOD

1.Heat the oil in a large saucepan over medium heat. Add onion, garlic,
ginger and coriander roots and stalks, and cook for 5 minutes or until soft.
Add curry paste and palm sugar, and cook for 1-2 minutes or until fragrant.
Add lentils, stock and three-quarters coconut milk. Bring to the boil, reduce
to a simmer and cook for 30 minutes or until lentils are tender and starting
to break down. Remove from heat and stir through coriander leaves, fish
sauce and lime juice. Season.
2.Divide among serving bowls and drizzle over remaining 100ml coconut
milk. Scatter over chilli, coconut, if using, and extra coriander leaves to
serve.

Creamy pumpkin soup

INGREDIENTS

2 tablespoons olive oil, plus extra to serve
1 onion, roughly chopped
2 garlic cloves, roughly chopped
600g pumpkin, peeled, chopped
1 potato, chopped
2 carrots, chopped
1 leek (white part only), chopped
1/2 teaspoon ground nutmeg
3 cups (750ml) Massel Chicken Style Liquid Stock
1/2 cup (125ml) pure (thin) cream
1 tablespoon pumpkin seeds (pepitas), toasted
Dried cranberries, to serve
Finely chopped flat-leaf parsley leaves, to serve

METHOD

1.Heat oil in a large saucepan over medium heat. Add onion and cook for 2-3 minutes until soft. Add garlic, vegetables and nutmeg, then toss to coat. Add stock and 2 cups (500ml) water, then bring to the boil. Reduce heat to low, cover and cook for 25 minutes or until the vegetables are tender. Cool slightly.
2.In batches, transfer to a blender and whiz until smooth. Return soup to the saucepan and place over low heat. Stir in cream, then season. To serve, ladle into bowls and top with seeds, cranberries and parsley, then drizzle with extra oil.

Corn soup with pan-fried mushrooms

INGREDIENTS

12 fresh corn cobs
140g unsalted butter, chopped
10 large eschalots (350g total), halved, thinly sliced
1 cup (250ml) pure (thin) cream
200g mixed mushrooms (such as Swiss brown, chestnut or pine mushrooms),
halved or chopped if large
1 garlic clove, finely chopped
1/2 long red chilli, seeds removed, finely chopped
1/4 cup chopped chives
Truffle oil (see note) or extra virgin olive oil, to serve

METHOD

1.Remove the husk and silks from the corn, then cut the kernels from the cobs. Set kernels aside, then cut the corn cobs in half. Place cobs and 4L water in a large saucepan, bring to the boil over medium heat and boil rapidly for 1 hour. Drain the corn stock and discard cobs; you should have about 1.25-1.5L corn stock.

2.Heat 100g butter in a large saucepan over low heat, add eschalots and cook, stirring occasionally, for 10 minutes or until soft. Add corn kernels and cook, stirring frequently, for 15 minutes or until tender. Add corn stock, bring to the boil, then simmer for 15 minutes. Stir in cream, season, then puree using a stick blender, or in batches in a blender, until smooth.

3.Heat remaining 40g butter in a large frypan over high heat, add mushrooms, garlic and chilli, and cook, tossing, for 5 minutes or until tender and browned.

4.Spoon the mushrooms into the centre of wide, shallow bowls, then ladle the soup around. Scatter with the chives, drizzle with truffle oil, then serve.

Corn soup with chive oil

INGREDIENTS

1/4 cup finely chopped chives
1/2 cup (125ml) olive oil
6 fresh corn cobs, husks removed
1 onion, finely chopped
1 celery stalk, finely chopped, plus extra 1/4 cup very finely chopped celery
2 garlic cloves, crushed
3 desiree potatoes, peeled, chopped
2 cups (500ml) chicken stock or water

METHOD

1.Blend chives with 1/3 cup (80ml) oil and 1 ice cube until smooth. Chill until needed.
2.Cut kernels from cobs, reserve cobs.
3.Heat the remaining oil in a large pan over medium heat. Cook onion, celery and garlic for 5 minutes or until soft. Add the kernels and potato, and cook for 1 minute. Add the stock, cobs and 1 litre water. Bring to the boil, then simmer over medium-low heat for 30 minutes or until potato is tender. Discard the cobs and blend soup until smooth. Strain through a fine sieve, season and serve topped with chive oil and extra celery.

Ham and red lentil soup

INGREDIENTS

2 tbs olive oil, plus 2 tbs extra
1 onion, finely chopped
1 carrot, finely chopped
2 celery sticks, finely chopped
3 garlic cloves, crushed
3 sprigs thyme, leaves chopped, plus 3 sprigs extra
3 sprigs sage, leaves chopped
375g (2 cups and 2 tbs) red lentils
250g piece smoked ham

METHOD

1.Heat oil in a large saucepan over medium heat, add onion, carrot and celery, and cook, stirring occasionally, for 5 minutes. Add garlic and herbs, cook for a further minute or until fragrant, then add 8 cups (2 litres) water, lentils and ham, season and cook, stirring occasionally, for 45 minutes. Remove ham from saucepan, cool for 10 minutes, then roughly shred and return three-quarters to the saucepan (reserve remaining) and stir to combine.

2.For garnish, heat extra oil in a small saucepan over medium-high heat, add extra sage and thyme and cook for 2 minutes or until crisp. Drain on paper towel, reserving oil, and season with salt.

3.Divide soup among serving bowls and scatter with remaining shredded ham, crisp herbs and reserved oil.

Ham and red lentil soup

INGREDIENTS

2 tbs olive oil, plus 2 tbs extra
1 onion, finely chopped
1 carrot, finely chopped
2 celery sticks, finely chopped
3 garlic cloves, crushed
3 sprigs thyme, leaves chopped, plus 3 sprigs extra
3 sprigs sage, leaves chopped
375g (2 cups and 2 tbs) red lentils
250g piece smoked ham

METHOD

1.Heat oil in a large saucepan over medium heat, add onion, carrot and celery, and cook, stirring occasionally, for 5 minutes. Add garlic and herbs, cook for a further minute or until fragrant, then add 8 cups (2 litres) water, lentils and ham, season and cook, stirring occasionally, for 45 minutes. Remove ham from saucepan, cool for 10 minutes, then roughly shred and return three-quarters to the saucepan (reserve remaining) and stir to combine.

2.For garnish, heat extra oil in a small saucepan over medium-high heat, add extra sage and thyme and cook for 2 minutes or until crisp. Drain on paper towel, reserving oil, and season with salt.

3.Divide soup among serving bowls and scatter with remaining shredded ham, crisp herbs and reserved oil.

Coconut fish noodle soup

INGREDIENTS

2 tbs coconut oil
2 garlic cloves, crushed
1 tbs ginger, finely grated
2 shallots, thinly sliced
1/4 cup (60g) Thai red curry paste, or to taste
600ml coconut milk
2 tbs crunchy peanut butter
1/4 cup (60ml) fish sauce
3 kaffir lime leaves, plus extra very thinly sliced to serve
2 tsp brown sugar
600g skinless firm white fish fillet, cut into 4cm pieces (we used ling)
3 baby bok choy, leaves seperated
Juice of 1 lime, plus wedges to serve
200g rice vermicelli noodles, cooked according to packet instructions
Coriander, to serve
Thai basil, to serve
Thinly sliced red onion, to serve
Red chilli, to serve
Toasted coconut flakes, to serve

METHOD

1.Heat oil in a large saucepan and fry garlic, ginger and shallot, stirring occasionally, for 2 minutes or until soft. Add paste and cook, stirring regularly, for 3 minutes or until fragrant. Add 1 cup (250ml) water, coconut milk, peanut butter, fish sauce, kaffir lime leaves and sugar, stir to combine, bring to a simmer and cook for 5 minutes. Add fish, cook for 3 minutes or until just cooked through, adding bok choy in last minute, then stir in lime juice.

2.Divide noodles among serving bowls and spoon in fish, bok choy and broth. Top with herbs, onion, chilli, coconut and kaffir lime leaf.

Lentil, pancetta and spinach soup

INGREDIENTS

1 tablespoon olive oil
1 onion, finely chopped
2 celery stalks, finely chopped
1cm-thick piece pancetta (100g), chopped
2 garlic cloves, crushed
2 cups (500ml) low-salt chicken stock
400g can brown lentils, rinsed, drained
2 vine-ripened tomatoes, chopped
1 bunch English spinach, stalks trimmed, thinly sliced
3 tablespoons (1/4 cup) shaved parmesan

METHOD

1.Heat the oil in a large saucepan over medium heat. Cook onion, celery and pancetta for 6-7 minutes, stirring occasionally, until pancetta is slightly crisp. Add the garlic and cook, stirring, for 30 seconds. Stir in stock, 2 cups (500ml) water, lentils and tomato, then bring to the boil. Reduce heat to low and simmer for 5 minutes.
2.Remove from the heat, add spinach and stir until just wilted. Season with sea salt and freshly ground black pepper. Divide among bowls, then serve scattered with parmesan and a little more pepper.

Lemongrass chicken and rice soup

INGREDIENTS

1.2kg whole chicken
1.5L (6 cups) Massel Chicken Style Liquid Stock
2 lemongrass stalks (inner core only), halved lengthways
5cm piece (25g) ginger, thinly sliced
250g microwave basmati rice
Coriander leaves, micro shiso & chopped pickled chilli (from Asian food shops), to serve
SPRING ONION AND CORIANDER SAUCE
1 tbs finely grated ginger
4 spring onions, finely sliced
1/3 cup (80ml) sunflower oil
2 tbs chopped coriander leaves

METHOD

1.Place the chicken, breast-side down, on a chopping board. Using sharp kitchen scissors or poultry shears, cut down either side of the backbone to remove. Discard (or freeze to use in stock). Then, using a sharp knife, halve the chicken down the breastbone.
2.Place chicken, stock, lemongrass and ginger in a large saucepan with a lid over high heat, adding extra stock or water, if necessary, to cover the chicken. Cover and bring to the boil. Reduce heat to a slow boil and cook, covered, for 10 minutes. Remove from heat and stand, covered, for 10 minutes or until chicken is cooked through. (The juices of the chicken will run clear when the thickest part of a thigh is pierced with a skewer.)
3.Meanwhile, for the spring onion and coriander sauce, combine ginger, spring onion and 1 tsp sea salt in a heatproof bowl. Heat oil in a saucepan over high heat for 1-2 minutes or until surface of oil begins to shimmer slightly. Carefully pour hot oil over the spring onion mixture and stir to combine. Stand for 5 minutes to cool slightly, then stir through coriander.
4.Heat the basmati rice according to the packet instructions.
5.Using a slotted spoon, transfer chicken pieces to a chopping board and halve crossways. Divide rice, soup and chicken among serving bowls and top with coriander and micro shiso. Serve with pickled chilli and sauce.

Leek and yoghurt soup with slow-braised onions

INGREDIENTS

500g natural yoghurt
1 tbs olive oil
80g unsalted butter
4 large onions, thinly sliced
1 star anise
2 leeks, trimmed, sliced into 1cm rounds
3 spring onions, thinly sliced
1 tsp plain flour
2 cups (500ml) vegetable stock 1 tsp dried mint
1/2 tsp ground turmeric
1/2 tsp of curry powder
1/4 cup of currants, soaked in boiling water
1/2 cup toasted walnuts, roughly chopped
Dill sprigs and mint leaves, to serve

METHOD

1.Place a large sieve over a bowl, ensuring it doesn't touch the base. Line with muslin or a clean Chux, leaving enough overhanging the sides to cover. Place yoghurt in sieve, draw muslin over the top and chill for at least 1 hour to remove some of the whey and create what the Afghanis call chaka.

2.Meanwhile, heat oil and half the butter in a heavy-based saucepan over low heat. Add onion and cook with star anise, stirring occasionally, for 15 minutes, then add leek and spring onion and cook, stirring, for a further 25 minutes or until onion is a lovely golden brown. Remove star anise and keep the onion mixture warm.

3.Mix the flour with a little stock to form a paste, then mix into the remaining stock- this will help thicken the soup and also stop it from splitting.

4.Whisk the yoghurt and the floured vegetable stock together and stir in the dried mint.

5.Pour the yoghurt mixture into a clean saucepan. Gently warm the soup over low heat and bring to a gentle simmer, but do not let it boil or it may split. Stir until slightly thickened and season well.

6.Meanwhile, in a small pan, warm remaining 40g butter with the turmeric and curry powder over medium heat until it foams. Immediately remove from heat and set aside.

7.Drain the currants and pat dry. To serve, divide the onion mixture between four warm serving bowls and top with currants, walnuts, dill and mint. Pour the warm yoghurt soup into the bowls and drizzle with a little of the warm curry butter.

Japanese tofu soup

INGREDIENTS

200g fresh shiitake mushrooms, halved
200g thick Korean glass noodles (see note) or thin glass noodles (bean thread vermicelli)
1/2 small Chinese cabbage, thickly sliced
4 spring onions, chopped, plus extra to serve
600g silken firm tofu (at room temperature), drained, cubed

BROTH

2L (8 cups) dashi (Japanese fish stock)(see note), made with dashi powder prepared to packet directions
3/4 cup (185ml) mirin (see note)
3/4 cup (185ml) reduced-salt soy sauce
1/4 cup (60ml) sake

METHOD

1.For the broth, combine all the ingredients in a large saucepan and bring to the boil. Simmer over medium heat for 5 minutes for flavours to develop.
2.Add mushrooms and noodles and simmer for 5 minutes. Add cabbage and spring onion and simmer for a further 2-3 minutes. Place the noodles and vegetables in bowls, top with cubed tofu and ladle over the broth. Garnish with extra spring onion and serve at once.

Japanese pumpkin and tofu soup

INGREDIENTS

1kg butternut pumpkin, peeled, cut into 1.5cm cubes
2 x 10g sachets instant dashi stock powder
1/4 cup (60ml) soy sauce
2 tablespoons mirin (Japanese rice wine)
100g silken firm tofu, cut into 1.5cm cubes
75g baby spinach leaves
200g mixed mushrooms (such as chestnut, shimeji and shiitake), trimmed, sliced if large
Sesame oil & toasted sesame seeds, to serve

METHOD

1.Place 1.5L (6 cups) lightly salted water in a large saucepan over medium heat.
2.Add the pumpkin, bring to a simmer, then cook for 10-15 minutes until tender but not too soft. Stir in the dashi powder, soy sauce and mirin. Add the tofu and simmer for 5 minutes or until warmed through.
3.Add the baby spinach and mushrooms and cook for 30 seconds until wilted. Remove from the heat.
4.Divide the soup among warmed serving bowls, then add a dash of sesame oil to taste, scatter with toasted sesame seeds and serve.

Japanese egg and pork curry soup

INGREDIENTS

8 cups (2L) beef stock
1 tbs sunflower oil
2 long green shallots, white part finely chopped, green part shredded
100g unsalted butter, chopped
2/3 cup (100g) plain flour
1 1/2 tbs curry powder
1 tbs each mirin and sake
1 tsp dark soy sauce
4 eggs, at room temperature
270g udon noodles, cooked according to packet instructions
Nori sheets and bonito flakes (optional – from Asian food shops), to serve
SAKE AND MIRIN PORK
2 tbs sunflower oil
500g pork mince
2cm piece (10g) ginger, finely grated
1 tbs each mirin and dark soy sauce
2 tbs sake, 2 tsp raw sugar

METHOD

1.To make the soup, heat stock in a saucepan over high heat until hot, then cover and set aside.

2.Meanwhile, heat oil in a second saucepan over medium-high heat. Add finely chopped shallot and cook, stirring regularly, for 3 minutes or until softened. Add butter and cook, stirring occasionally, until foaming. Add flour and cook, stirring constantly, for 3 minutes to cook flour through. Add curry powder and cook, stirring constantly, for 1 minute or until well combined. In 2 batches, gradually whisk hot stock into curry mixture. Bring to a simmer, stir through mirin, sake and soy, reduce heat to low and cover to keep hot.

3.Meanwhile, for the sake and mirin pork, heat oil in a frypan over high heat. Add pork and ginger, and cook, breaking up mince with a wooden spoon, for 4 minutes or until browned. Add remaining ingredients and cook, stirring occasionally, for 3 minutes or until reduced slightly.

4.To cook the eggs, bring a saucepan of water to the boil, carefully add eggs and cook for 6 minutes 30 seconds for a soft-set yolk, or until cooked to your liking. Immediately drain and transfer to a bowl of iced water. When cool enough to handle, peel and stand in iced water until needed.

5.Bring soup back to the boil. Divide noodles and soup among serving bowls. Top with pork mixture, halved eggs, shredded shallot, nori and bonito, if using, to serve.

Italian fish soup with white beans

INGREDIENTS

1/4 cup (60ml) olive oil, plus extra to drizzle
1 onion, thinly sliced
2 celery stalks, thinly sliced
3 garlic cloves, thinly sliced
1 red capsicum, sliced 1cm thick
400g can Ardmona Diced Tomatoes
500ml Ardmona Pureed Tomatoes (sugo: see Notes)
Good pinch of dried red chilli flakes
2 rosemary sprigs
2 bay leaves
1 cup (250ml) vegetable stock or water
1 teaspoon paprika
400g can cannellini beans, rinsed, drained
250g punnet cherry tomatoes
800g skinless fish fillets, cut in 4cm pieces (see Notes)
8 tiger prawns, peeled (tails intact)
16-20 mussels, scrubbed, debearded
Chopped flat-leaf parsley, to serve

METHOD

1.Heat the oil in a wide saucepan over medium heat. Fry the onion, celery and garlic for 5 minutes, stirring occasionally, until soft.
2.Add capsicum, tomatoes, passata, chilli, herbs, stock and paprika. Season. Simmer over medium-low heat, partly covered, for 20 minutes until capsicum softens.
3.Add the beans and cherry tomatoes and cook for 5 minutes or until tomatoes soften.
4.Add the seafood. Cover and simmer gently for 4-5 minutes until mussels have opened and the fish and prawns are just cooked. Discard any mussels that haven't opened after this time.
5.Season to taste, then divide among bowls and serve immediately, garnished with parsley and drizzled with olive oil.

Hot and sour soup

INGREDIENTS

4 dried shiitake mushrooms (see Notes)
1L (4 cups) chicken stock
200g pork fillet, cut into thin strips
5cm piece ginger, peeled, cut into thin matchsticks
2 tablespoons canned bamboo shoots, rinsed
2 spring onions, trimmed, thinly sliced
250g firm tofu, chopped
1 tablespoon cornflour
2 tablespoons each soy sauce and rice vinegar
1/2 teaspoon sesame oil
Chilli oil, to serve (optional)
1/2 teaspoon white pepper

METHOD

1.Soak the shiitakes in warm water for 30 minutes. Drain, then remove and discard stems and thinly slice the caps.
2.Bring the stock to a simmer over medium heat in a large saucepan. Add the pork, mushrooms, ginger, bamboo shoots and 1/2 teaspoon salt and simmer for 2 minutes, skimming. Add tofu and simmer for 2 minutes.
3.Mix the cornflour with soy sauce and vinegar and add gradually to the soup, stirring continuously. Stir in 1/2 teaspoon white pepper.
4.Top with spring onion and serve drizzled with sesame oil, and chilli oil if desired.

Hot and sour prawn soup

INGREDIENTS

250g rice stick noodles
1.5L (6 cups) chicken stock
1-2 tablespoons green curry paste to taste
1 tablespoon soy sauce
1 tablespoon caster sugar
Juice of 1 lime
2 tomatoes, chopped
2 celery stalks, sliced
20 green prawns, peeled (tails intact), deveined
Sliced red chilli, bean sprouts, coriander and mint leaves, to serve

METHOD

1.Soak rice stick noodles in boiling water according to packet instructions. Drain and set aside.
2.Place chicken stock, green curry paste to taste, soy sauce, sugar and lime juice in a large pan and bring to the boil. Add tomatoes and celery stalks. Reduce heat to medium-low. Simmer for 5 minutes until tomatoes have softened slightly. Add prawns, then cook for 2-3 minutes until just cooked through.
3.Divide noodles among bowls. Spoon soup and prawns over. Serve with chilli, bean sprouts, coriander and mint leaves.

Hot and sour noodle soup with prawns

INGREDIENTS

2 kaffir lime leaves
2 cups (500ml) chicken stock
2 small red chillies, seeds removed, finely chopped
3cm-piece ginger, peeled, thinly sliced
2 tbs fish sauce
1 tbs tamarind paste
200g glass (bean thread) noodles or rice vermicelli
150g green beans or snake beans, trimmed, cut into 3cm lengths
12 cherry tomatoes, halved
16 large green king prawns, peeled (tails intact), deveined
Coriander sprigs and lime cheeks (optional), to serve

METHOD

1.Place the stock, kaffir lime leaves, chilli, ginger, fish sauce, tamarind paste and 2 cups (500ml) water in a large heavy-based saucepan, and bring to the boil over high heat. Reduce heat to medium-low and simmer for 5 minutes.
2.Meanwhile, place the glass noodles or vermicelli in a large heatproof bowl and pour over enough boiling water to cover. Set aside for 3 minutes to soften, then rinse and drain well and divide among serving bowls.
3.Add the green or snake beans to the soup and simmer for a further 2 minutes. Add the tomatoes and prawns, then remove from the heat. Stand for 1 minute until prawns are just cooked, then ladle soup over the noodles and garnish with coriander sprigs. Serve immediately, with lime cheeks if desired.

Hot and sour noodle soup with minced chicken

INGREDIENTS

2 teaspoons sunflower oil
250g lean chicken mince
1 bunch broccolini, trimmed, cut on the diagonal
1L (4 cups) chicken stock
2 garlic cloves, thinly sliced
1 long red chilli, sliced on an angle
12 green king prawns, peeled (tails intact), deveined
2 tablespoons fish sauce
1 tablespoon caster sugar
2 tablespoons lime juice, plus wedges to serve
1/2 cup coriander leaves
1/4 cup mint leaves
100g flat rice noodles
1 tablespoon chopped unsalted roasted peanuts
Chilli powder, to serve

METHOD

1.Heat oil in a frypan over medium-high heat. Add chicken and cook, stirring, for 2-3 minutes until browned and cooked through. Season and set aside.

2.Blanch broccolini in boiling salted water for 3 minutes or until tender. Drain and refresh under cold water. Set aside.

3.Combine stock, garlic and sliced chilli in a pan and bring to the boil. Add prawns, fish sauce and sugar, then cook over medium heat for 1-2 minutes until prawns are opaque. Add broccolini and cook for 1-2 minutes to warm through, then stir through lime juice and most of the herbs.

4.Meanwhile, cook noodles according to the packet instructions. Drain, then divide among 4 serving bowls.

5.Remove prawns and broccolini from the broth with a slotted spoon and arrange on top of the noodles. Top with chicken, then ladle over broth. Scatter over peanuts, chilli powder and remaining herbs, then serve immediately with a lime wedge

Chicken noodle soup

INGREDIENTS

1.6kg whole chicken
2 onions, quartered
2 bay leaves
2 leeks (pale part only), thinly sliced
2 parsnips, peeled, sliced
2 carrots, halved, thinly sliced
2 celery stalks, thinly sliced
50g baby spinach leaves
170g thin dried egg noodles
2 tablespoons flat-leaf parsley leaves
2 tablespoons dill sprigs

METHOD

1.Rinse chicken and pat dry with paper towel. Place in a large stockpot and add 2 1/2L (10 cups) cold water. Add onion and bay leaves (top with a saucer to keep chicken submerged). Bring to the boil over medium-high heat. Reduce heat to medium and cook, skimming impurities from the surface, for 30 minutes or until cooked through.

2.Remove chicken from pan. Carve off the breast fillets either side of the breast bone, remove and discard skin and set aside.

3.Return the chicken carcass to the pot, add the leek, parsnip, carrot and celery, then season. Cook for a further 30 minutes or until the vegetables are tender.

4.Remove chicken from the pot, and shred the remaining meat from legs and thighs, discarding skin. Shred meat from the reserved breast fillets.

5.Return shredded chicken to the pan with spinach leaves. Cook, stirring, for 5 minutes or until warmed through.

6.Meanwhile, cook the noodles according to packet instructions. Drain.

7.Divide the noodles among bowls, ladle over the soup, then garnish with parsley and dill sprigs to serve.

Ham hock and lentil soup

INGREDIENTS

1 tbs olive oil
2 carrots, finely chopped
1 leek (white part only), thinly sliced
1 celeriac bulb, peeled, finely chopped or 2 celery stalks, finely chopped
4-5 garlic cloves, crushed
200g red lentils, rinsed, drained
1/2 tsp grated nutmeg
750g ham hock
2L (8 cups) chicken or vegetable stock
PARSLEY AND MINT PESTO
2 tbs finely chopped flat-leaf parsley leaves
1 tbs finely chopped mint
1/2 cup (50g) grated parmesan
2 tbs extra virgin olive oil

METHOD

1.Heat oil in a large stockpot or saucepan, add carrot, leek, celeriac and garlic, and cook over medium-low heat, stirring, for 3-4 minutes until softened. Add lentils and cook, stirring, for 30 seconds, then stir in nutmeg. Add hock and stock, bring to the boil, then reduce heat to low. Cover pan with a lid and allow soup to simmer for 2 hours.
2.Meanwhile, make the pesto by pounding all ingredients in a mortar and pestle (or combine in a small food processor) until mixture forms a small paste. Season with pepper.
3.Remove hock from soup, remove and discard skin and fat, and cut meat into small, bite-sized pieces. To serve, pour soup into 6 serving bowls, add ham pieces and drizzle with pesto.
4.Accompany with crusty bread.

French onion soup with gruyere puff tops

INGREDIENTS

15g dried porcini mushrooms, finely chopped
2 tbs extra virgin olive oil
50g unsalted butter
5 onions, thinly sliced
3 garlic cloves, crushed
4 sprigs thyme, leaves picked
150ml white wine
1 cup (250ml) beer (we used a golden ale)
1L chicken stock
2 sheets puff pastry
1 egg, lightly beaten
200g gruyere cheese, grated
Flat-leaf parsley leaves to serve

METHOD

1.Preheat oven to 200°C. Place mushrooms in a heatproof bowl and pour over 500ml hot water and set aside until needed.
2.Heat oil and butter in a saucepan over medium-low heat. Add onions, season with salt and cook 15 minutes until softened. Add garlic and thyme and cook for 5 minutes until fragrant. Increase heat to medium-high and add the wine and beer. Bring to a simmer and cook for 3-4 minutes.
3.Add the mushrooms and mushroom liquid as well as the chicken stock. Continue to simmer for 10 minutes for the flavours to infuse.
4.Meanwhile, cut puff pastry into 4 rounds to roughly match size of the soup dishes. Place on a lined baking tray and brush with egg. Bake 10-12 minutes until puffed, then top with the cheese and baking for 5 minutes or until golden. Remove from the oven and cool slightly.
5.Season soup to taste, then divide between 4 bowls. Serve with gruyere puff tops and parsley.

Pea and pea shoot soup with coriander and sweet chilli cream

INGREDIENTS

2 tablespoons olive oil
20g unsalted butter
1/2 teaspoon ground cumin
2 teaspoons grated ginger
1 onion, finely chopped
1 potato, peeled, chopped
1/2 bunch coriander, stems cleaned and chopped, leaves picked
500g frozen peas
50g pea shoots, plus extra to garnish
3 cups (750ml) chicken stock
2 tablespoons sweet chilli sauce
200ml creme fraiche or sour cream
Juice of 1 lemon

METHOD

1.Heat oil and butter in a large pan over low heat. Add cumin and ginger and stir for a few seconds until fragrant. Add onion, potato and coriander stems and cook, adding a little water occasionally to keep vegetables from catching, for 5 minutes. Add peas, shoots, stock and coriander leaves. Bring to the boil, then simmer over low heat for 3 minutes.
2.Meanwhile, swirl sweet chilli sauce through the creme fraiche or sour cream.
3.Remove soup from heat, then use a stick blender to puree soup until smooth (or cool slightly, then puree in batches in a blender and return to pan). Warm over low heat, then season and stir in lemon juice.
4.Ladle soup into bowls. Top with a swirl of sweet chilli cream and extra pea shoots.

Pea and ham soup with salami bites

INGREDIENTS

50g unsalted butter
1 onion, finely chopped
225g potatoes, chopped
900ml chicken stock
350g frozen peas
100g Primo Honey-Cured Leg Ham, thinly sliced
150ml thickened cream, plus extra to serve
1 tablespoon chopped flat-leaf parsley
1 tablespoon chopped mint
SALAMI BITES
2 sheets puff pastry
1 tablespoon basil pesto or sun-dried tomato pesto
100g Primo Hungarian Salami

METHOD

1.Melt the butter in a saucepan over low heat. Add onion and cook until soft. Add potatoes and cook, stirring, for 1-2 minutes. Add stock and cook for 10 minutes or until potatoes are soft.
2.Add peas, bring to the boil and cook for 3 minutes. Process in a blender until smooth. Stir in half the ham, and season with salt and pepper. Stir in cream and herbs, then heat through.
3.Meanwhile, to make salami bites, preheat the oven to 180°C.
4.Lay pastry on a baking sheet lined with baking paper. Prick the pastry base all over with a fork and bake for 5 minutes.
5.Remove from oven and spread with pesto. Lay salami in overlapping slices over pesto. Bake for a further 10 minutes or until golden. Remove from the oven, slice each sheet in half then cut into 3cm strips.
6.Serve the soup with extra cream, garnish with remaining ham and season with pepper. Serve with salami bites.

Parsnip and leek soup with roasted garlic and thyme oil

INGREDIENTS

1 garlic bulb
140ml extra virgin olive oil
4 parsnips, peeled
3 leeks (white part only), thinly sliced
3 bay leaves
1.5L (6 cups) chicken or vegetable stock
1/2 cup thyme leaves
1/4 cup (35g)

METHOD

1.Preheat oven to 200°C. Place garlic on a piece of foil, drizzle with 1 tbs oil and wrap to enclose. Place on a baking tray and roast for 40 minutes or until very soft.

2.Squeeze garlic from cloves and set aside. While garlic is cooking, cut one parsnip into matchsticks. Place on a baking tray lined with baking paper and drizzle with 1/4 cup (60ml) oil. Season.

3.Bake for 18 minutes or until golden. Set aside. Meanwhile, heat 2 tbs oil in a large pan over medium-low heat.

4.Cook leek, stirring occasionally, for 20 minutes or until very soft. Chop remaining parsnips and add to pan with bay.

5.Cook, stirring, for 2 minutes or until coated. Add stock, increase heat to high and bring to the boil. Reduce heat to medium-low and simmer for 40 minutes or until parsnip is very tender. Remove bay and cool slightly.

6.Using a stick blender, blend until smooth. Stir in garlic.

7.Heat remaining 1 tbs oil in a frypan over medium heat. Add thyme leaves, stir to coat, then immediately remove from heat. Serve soup topped with parsnip chips, hazelnuts and drizzle with thyme oil

Pappa al pomodoro (tomato and bread soup)

INGREDIENTS

1 tablespoon olive oil
1 small onion, finely chopped
2 garlic cloves, thinly sliced
3 x 400g cans whole tomatoes
2 cups (500ml) vegetable stock
Half a day-old ciabatta loaf, cut into 3cm cubes
1/2 cup basil leaves, torn if large
Shaved parmesan, to serve

METHOD

1.Heat the olive oil in a saucepan over medium-low heat. Cook the onion, stirring, for 5-7 minutes until translucent. Add the garlic and cook, stirring, for 1 minute.

2.Roughly chop tomatoes from 2 of the cans, reserving juice. Add all tomatoes and their juices to the pan. Bring to the boil over high heat, then reduce heat to medium and simmer for 5 minutes. Add stock, bread and 1 cup (250ml) water. Simmer for 2 minutes until thickened. Remove from heat and stir in basil, reserving some to garnish, then season to taste with salt and pepper. Serve at once topped with parmesan and reserved basil.

Panzanella soup

INGREDIENTS

410g can chopped tomatoes
1 green capsicum, seeded, chopped
1/2 telegraph cucumber, peeled, seeded, chopped
1 small red onion, chopped, plus extra slices to garnish
1 garlic clove, crushed
1 tablespoon red wine vinegar
1 tablespoon extra virgin olive oil
200ml tomato juice
6 black olives, pitted, sliced
1 tablespoon salted capers, rinsed
2 tablespoons small basil leaves
Toasted croutons, to serve

METHOD

1.Place the tomatoes, capsicum, cucumber, onion, garlic, vinegar, olive oil and tomato juice in a blender, and process to combine.
2.Add enough water to make a thickish soup consistency, then season with salt and pepper. Refrigerate until ready to serve. Toss together the olives, capers, basil leaves and croutons, and serve on top of the soup.

Oxtail, silverbeet and chickpea soup with parmesan dippers

INGREDIENTS

2 tbs extra virgin olive oil, plus extra to serve
2kg oxtail, thickly sliced, 2 tsp fennel seeds
1 tsp dried chilli flakes, 1 leek, trimmed, chopped
1 each onion, celery stalk and carrot, chopped
2 bay leaves, 4 garlic cloves, crushed
1 tsp finely chopped rosemary leaves
1 parmesan rind (optional), 4 cups (1L) chicken stock
400g can whole tomatoes, 1/2 bunch silverbeet, stalks removed, leaves chopped
Basil leaves, shaved fennel and fennel fronds (optional), to serve

PARMESAN DIPPERS

50g finely grated parmesan
50g unsalted butter, softened
1/2 tsp fennel seeds, crushed
1/4 tsp dried chilli flakes
1/2 baguette, thinly sliced

METHOD

1.Heat oil in a large saucepan over medium-high heat. In batches, add oxtail and cook, turning halfway, for 6 minutes or until browned. Transfer to a bowl. Remove from heat and drain all but 2 tbs fat from the pan, then return to mediumhigh heat. Add fennel seeds and chilli flakes, and cook, stirring constantly, for 30 seconds or until fragrant. Add leek, onion, celery and carrot, and cook, stirring occasionally, for 6 minutes or until softened. Add bay leaves, garlic and rosemary, and cook, stirring constantly, for 1 minute or until fragrant. Add the parmesan rind, if using, stock, tomatoes, 2 cups (500ml) water and oxtail. Bring to a simmer, reduce heat to low, cover and cook, stirring twice, for 3 hours or until oxtail is very tender.

2.In final 20 minutes of oxtail cooking time, for the parmesan dippers, combine parmesan, butter, fennel and chilli flakes in a bowl. Spread over one side of baguette and place, buttered-side up, on prepared tray. Bake for 10 minutes or until golden.

3.Skim and discard layer of fat from top of soup, then add the silverbeet. Increase heat to medium-high and simmer, stirring occasionally, for 3 minutes or until silverbeet is wilted.

4.Divide soup among serving bowls, drizzle with extra oil and top with basil and fennel. Serve with parmesan dippers scattered with fennel fronds, if using.

Mussels, leek and saffron soup

INGREDIENTS

1.5kg small mussels, scrubbed, beards removed
1/4 cup (60ml) dry white wine
2 leeks (white party only – to give about 450g)
75g unsalted butter
1 small onion, finely chopped
2 tbs plain flour
450ml good-quality fish stock*
Good pinch of saffron threads
50ml thickened cream

METHOD

1.Place the mussels and wine in a large pan. Cover and cook over high heat for 2-3 minutes, shaking the pan every now and then until the mussels have opened, discarding any mussels that don't open after this time. Tip them into a colander set over a bowl (to collect the liquid) and leave to cool slightly. Remove the mussels from all but 8 of the nicest-looking shells, then set all the mussels aside until ready to serve.

2.From the white part of the leek, cut one 5cm-long piece into matchsticks. Finely chop the rest. Melt the butter in a pan over medium-low heat, add the chopped leeks and the onion and cook gently for 3-4 minutes until soft but not browned.

3.Stir in the flour and cook gently for 1 minute. Gradually stir in the strained mussel liquid and the stock, then bring to the boil, stirring. Add the saffron, reduce the heat to low and leave to simmer for 25 minutes.

4.Meanwhile, drop the leek matchsticks into a pan of boiling salted water, bring back to the boil, then drain and refresh under cold running water. Set aside until ready to serve.

Mushroom and potato soup with croutons and cucumber pickle

INGREDIENTS

20g dried porcini mushrooms, broken into pieces
1/2 cup (125ml) olive oil
30g unsalted butter
400g Swiss brown mushrooms, sliced
150g bacon, chopped
1 leek, finely chopped
2 garlic cloves, finely chopped
400g can chopped tomatoes
1L (4 cups) chicken stock
300g desiree potatoes, sliced
150g sourdough bread
1/2 bunch dill, sprigs chopped
1 Lebanese cucumber, thinly sliced into long ribbons, sliced into long matchsticks
1 tsp white wine vinegar
1/2 tsp caster sugar

METHOD

1. Preheat oven to 200°C. Place porcini mushrooms in a bowl with 1 cup (250ml) hot water, then set aside for 10 minutes.
2. Heat 1 tbs oil and half the butter in a frypan over medium-high heat. Add half the Swiss brown mushrooms, season and cook for 3-4 minutes until browned, then remove and set aside. Repeat with remaining butter, mushrooms and 1 tbs oil.
3. Heat another 1 tbs oil in the pan and cook the bacon for 3-4 minutes until crisp, then add leek and garlic, and cook for a further 2-3 minutes until softened. Add tomatoes and cook for a further 7 minutes or until reduced. Add stock, potato, Swiss brown mushrooms and porcini mushrooms and soaking liquid. Simmer for 10 minutes or until tender. Season to taste.
4. Drizzle bread with remaining 1/4 cup (60ml) olive oil. Scatter with dill and season with salt. Place on a baking tray and bake for 10 minutes or until golden.
5. For pickle, combine cucumber, vinegar, sugar and 1/2 tsp salt. Stand for 5 minutes.
6. Serve soup with pickle and croutons.

Moroccan harira soup

INGREDIENTS

1/2 cup (100g) dried chickpeas
1/4 cup (50g) dried yellow split peas
1/4 teaspoon saffron threads
2 tablespoons extra virgin olive oil
1 onion, finely chopped
1/4 teaspoon coriander seeds
1 teaspoon ground cumin
1/2 teaspoon ground cinnamon
1/2 bunch coriander, 3 roots finely chopped, leaves roughly chopped
2 lamb shank or leg bones (with some meat left on), halved (ask your butcher to cut)
2 x 400g canned chopped tomatoes
1 carrot, cut into 1cm cubes
1L (4 cups) chicken stock
1/4 cup (50g) whole green (Puy) lentils (see note)
1 tablespoon lemon juice
Lebanese bread, to serve

METHOD

1.Soak chickpeas and split peas in separate bowls of cold water overnight. The next day, drain pulses well and set aside.

2.Soak the saffron in 1 tablespoon hot water for 5 minutes. Heat olive oil in a large saucepan over medium heat. Add onion and cook for 3 minutes until slightly softened. Add spices, coriander root, and saffron and its liquid. Cook for 2-3 minutes until fragrant. Add bones, tomato, carrot, stock and 2 cups (500ml) water. Bring to the boil, then reduce heat to medium-low and simmer, covered, for 3 hours.

3.Uncover, add chickpeas and cook for 15 minutes, then add split peas and lentils and cook for a further 25-30 minutes or until pulses are tender. Remove bones (any meat should fall off by this time). Stir in juice and most of the coriander leaves, reserving some to garnish. Season, then serve with reserved coriander and bread.

Miso soup with tofu and snow peas

INGREDIENTS

1 1/2 tablespoons instant dashi (or enough to combine with 1L water
according to packet instructions)
2 tablespoons white (shiro) miso paste
100g snow peas, trimmed
200g silken firm tofu, drained
1 tablespoon mirin
1 tablespoon soy sauce

METHOD

1.Place dashi in a pan with 1 litre (4 cups) boiling water and stir for 2 minutes
over medium heat. Place miso paste in a bowl and add a ladleful of broth,
whisking to get rid of lumps. Slowly pour mixture back into pan, whisking
constantly.
2.Thinly slice the snow peas and cut the tofu into 2cm cubes. Add both to the
broth with the mirin and soy sauce and heat through gently without boiling.
3.Serve in small bowls.

Mexican seafood soup

INGREDIENTS

1/4 cup (60ml) olive oil
500g good-quality seafood marinara mix
1 teaspoon smoked paprika (pimenton) (see note)
1 onion, finely chopped
2 garlic cloves, sliced
1 red capsicum, thinly sliced
2 jalapeno or long green chillies, seeds removed, finely chopped
1/2 teaspoon dried oregano
3 teaspoons ground coriander
3 teaspoons ground cumin
1 teaspoon chilli flakes (optional)
2 x 400g cans chopped tomatoes
500ml good-quality fish or chicken stock
2 corn cobs
Grated zest & juice of 1 lime
Sour cream, chopped avocado, coriander leaves & chargrilled tortillas, to serve

METHOD

1.Heat oil in a large pan over high heat. In a bowl toss the seafood with half the paprika, then season and cook, turning, for 2-3 minutes until seafood is lightly seared and just cooked. Remove seafood from pan and set aside.
2.Add onion to pan and cook, stirring, for 1-2 minutes until softened. Add garlic, capsicum, chilli, dried herbs, spices and remaining 1/2 teaspoon paprika and cook, stirring, for 2 minutes until soft. Reduce to medium-low heat, then add tomato and stock. Simmer for 12-15 minutes, stirring occasionally, until slightly thickened.
3.Cut kernels off corn cobs. Add kernels to soup with cooked seafood. Simmer for 2 minutes to heat through. Remove from heat and stir in lime zest and juice. Season.
4.Divide soup among 4 bowls and serve with sour cream, avocado, coriander and warm tortillas.

Little prawn soups

INGREDIENTS

2 tablespoons light olive oil
8 (about 250g) green king prawns, peeled (heads and shells reserved), deveined
200ml dry white wine
1 onion, finely chopped
2 celery stalks, thinly sliced
2 garlic cloves, thinly sliced
2 tablespoons tomato paste
1L (4 cups) fish stock or water
1/2 zucchini, very finely diced
1 tomato, very finely diced
1/2 cup tomato passata (sugo)
Pinch saffron threads
Pinch cayenne pepper
1/2 teaspoon sweet paprika
1 tablespoon finely chopped flat-leaf parsley
2 tablespoons thin cream (optional)

METHOD

1.Heat oil over high heat in a wide, heavy-based saucepan, and fry prawn heads and shells, stirring, for 3-4 minutes, mashing with a potato masher to squash them. Add wine and boil for 1 minute. Add onion, celery, garlic and paste, stir until well combined. Add stock, then bring to the boil and simmer rapidly over medium heat for 10 minutes. Strain through a fine sieve placed over a large pan, pressing down on the solids, then discard solids.

2.Reheat the broth and add the zucchini, tomato, passata, saffron, cayenne and paprika, and season to taste. Simmer, without boiling, over low heat for 5 minutes. Add the prawns and parsley, and cook for 2-3 minutes until cooked. Add the cream if you want a richer, bisque-like soup, and heat through.

Restorative lemongrass and chicken noodle soup

INGREDIENTS

1 x 1.4g whole chicken
3 tsp ground turmeric (we used Woolworths Macro)
2 lemongrass stalks, bruised
5cm piece (25g) ginger, peeled, sliced
1 onion (root intact), peeled, halved
6 kaffir limes leaves
1 bunch coriander, roots washed, trimmed, leaves reserved to serve
2 tsp coriander seeds, toasted
Juice of 1 lemon
3 tsp caster sugar
2 tbs light soy sauce
2 large garlic cloves, finely chopped
400g fresh egg noodles, cooked according to packet instructions
Indonesian sambal, Thai basil and toasted sesame seeds, to serve

METHOD

1.Place chicken, turmeric, lemongrass, ginger, onion, kaffir lime, coriander root and coriander seeds in a large stockpot. Cover with 3L cold water. Bring to a simmer, then cook for 50 minutes or until chicken is cooked through and stock is flavoursome.
2.Carefully transfer chicken to a plate. Cool, then carve into portions or shred. Stir lemon juice, sugar, soy and garlic through stock and remove from heat. Check seasoning and add more salt, sugar or garlic to taste. Divide noodles among serving bowls and ladle over soup.
3.Add chicken, sambal, Thai basil and reserved coriander leaves. Sprinkle over sesame seeds to serve.

Quick teriyaki chicken noodle soup

INGREDIENTS

270g udon noodles
130g white (shiro) miso paste (from Asian food shops)
200g shiitake mushrooms (larger mushrooms halved)
Thinly sliced spring onion and micro coriander, to serve
QUICK TERIYAKI
2 tbs Chinese black (chinkiang) vinegar (from Asian food shops)
2 tbs honey
1 tsp finely grated ginger
2 tsp white (shiro) miso paste
4 chicken thigh fillets (skin on)

METHOD

1.Cook noodles according to packet instructions. Drain and set aside.
2.Meanwhile, for the quick teriyaki, place all ingredients except chicken in a bowl and whisk until combined. Season with black pepper and add chicken. Set aside.
3.To make the soup, combine miso paste, shiitake and 1.5L (6 cups) water in a saucepan over medium-low heat and cook until heated through. Cover and keep warm over low heat.
4.Meanwhile, heat a chargrill pan to high heat. Thread 2 chicken thighs onto 2 skewers. Repeat with remaining chicken and skewers. Grill for 3-4 minutes each side or until cooked through. Remove from heat and rest for 5 minutes.
5.Remove chicken from skewers and cut into thick slices. Divide noodles and miso soup among bowls and top with chicken, spring onion and micro coriander to serve.

Pumpkin, pear and bacon soup

INGREDIENTS

80g unsalted butter, chopped
1 onion, chopped
150g bacon, chopped, plus extra 4 thin slices
3 pears (we used beurre bosc), 2 cored and chopped, 1 thinly sliced
1kg peeled butternut pumpkin, cut into 5cm pieces, seeds reserved
(substitute 1/3 cup [55g] store-bought pepitas)
4 cups (1L) Massel Chicken Style Liquid Stock
1 1/2 tsp sherry vinegar (substitute red wine vinegar)
1/2 bunch sage, leaves picked
2 tbs maple syrup

METHOD

1.Combine half the butter, onion, bacon and chopped pear in a large saucepan over medium heat. When hot, cook, stirring, for 8 minutes or until onion is softened.
2.Add pumpkin and stock, and bring to the boil. Reduce to a simmer and cook for 6 minutes or until pumpkin is tender. Working in batches, place mixture in a blender and whiz until smooth. Transfer to a saucepan, stir through vinegar and keep hot over low heat.
3.Meanwhile, place extra bacon in a frypan over medium-high heat. Cook for 2 minutes each side or until golden. Transfer to a bowl and set aside. Melt remaining 40g butter in pan. Add reserved pumpkin seeds and sage, and cook for 2 minutes or until seeds are golden.
4.Using a slotted spoon, transfer seeds to a plate. When sage darkens, transfer to a plate using tongs. Add maple syrup, sliced pear and 1/2 tsp salt flakes to pan. Cook pear for 1 1/2 - 2 minutes each side or until golden.
5.Divide soup among bowls and top with bacon, pear, sage and pumpkin seeds. Drizzle with pear cooking juices to serve.